Teen Rights and Freedoms

I Drugs